Nothing Lasts Forever

Na'Imah Laurent-Dixon

BookLeaf Publishing

Presentation by *BookLeaf Publishing*

Web: www.bookleafpub.com

E-mail: info@bookleafpub.com

ISBN: 9789395621182

First edition 2022

ACKNOWLEDGEMENT

Thank you to Letitia Chan, 'Foyle Young Poets of the Year Award', and The Poetry Society for allowing me to borrow some lines from 'Making Glutinous Dumplings with My Mother'. The borrowed lines are as follows:

"The kitchen drips with steam […] She puts balls of sesame
inside bigger folds of dough, white in her pale cracked palms.
Under the acrylic my mother's nails are short and small,
bent as umbrella tops. […]
I think of the dust that makes its way into the ball, the dead skin
of my hands. I make small nubs of dough. Sesame paste
sticks to the crevices of my mouth, […] When I am a mother I will also
dry my daughter's hair at two in the morning when she is limp
from sleeplessness and tears, […] my mother whom I envy and know because I too know how to be unwanted and androgynous, wordless in the way I am now,

in the way she goes on laughing. The ginger
tumbles in the pot.
My mother pours her dumplings into it and they
bubble
like bodies that have never belonged to us."

Find the poem here:

Chan, Letitia. "Making Glutinous Dumplings
with My Mother." in Painting You The
Darkness: Poems by Foyle Young Poets of the
Year 2016, The Poetry Society, 2016, p.17.

or online at:

https://poems.poetrysociety.org.uk/poems/makin
g-glutinous-dumplings-with-my-mother/

A special thank you to Rachel Cleverly at 'The
Poetry Society' for answering all of my emails
about whether or not I could use Letitia Chan's
poem in my own.

Tone-Deaf Haiku

An intuitive
gong undersea unheard by
strange landlocked ears. Tune.

In My Father's Garage

My books are swaddled
in puny bin-bags, piled high and weeping
themselves brown.
Past versions of me are pressed
between their pages – unbound,
making ghosts of the white space.

Nightmares

I rest my head on the cool side of my pillow
and tuck my feet under the covers to stop them
hanging
off my bed
like ropes.

Blck Lke

We are black like pens. Pen
like penitentiary, pen
like pentagram, pen
like penalised, pen
like penance.
All of these things are as black as
we:
Black-lists
Black-eyes
Black-face
Black-balled
Black like death
and black like funerals.
Black like iron chains
and black like iron bars.

Black like backgrounds.

Black like…

Sodium Lamp

5

If we waive our shine in death, your spirit is a
beam
roving through cosmic space – a ray
nine minutes before it dawns on us.
The chalky outline of your stiff body hovers
like a shorn halo on this unbroken
night. Its dim light cast into the silhouette
shaped hollow in lives
you did touch.
Limp petals won't eclipse the streetlight's pallid
flickering so I never lay flowers
at its base
for you.

(Do Not) Speak Ill of The Dead

The Priest shakes too much incense
over the brown blob
that is your coffin.
    wi did laughing and coughing at di same
time
    cuz him knows
The church fills with bitter
smoke, a mourner cracks
open a stained window.

We wait long enough for the cold to seep
through the soles
of our shoes.

Your daughters don't cry.
They read your eulogy from your legal pad,
sending a word to the court of God,
on your behalf.

    everybody did inna di pews a tell bad-mind
jokes bout yuh,
I hold my breath to keep from laughing.

Make It Make Sense

"It didn't bleed - but
I inspected my hand and
had blood tinged fingers."

Busting Joke

We puff gasped air from heaving chests, howling
so hard tears streak
down our cheeks, pooling into our mouths.
Our sodden teeth are soft-
bare without their enamel. We howl
so hard our diaphragms pop
and we start creasing,
soft folds of flesh folding
on top of each other.
We know how to bust joke until our sides split,
until our stitches sew us back together.

Fiery-Lights

9

I snake fairy-lights between the polaroids
I've Blu-Tacked to my wall. Later I admire my
twinkling exhibition.
Look at us, all frozen: in body-folding laughter,
powder coloured and glittering at J'ouvert,
mid banter eyes and lips semi-open. I linger
over a shot of both your hands braiding my hair.
I blink.

Darkness.

I blink fumbling for light. My phone's pale
searching
glow reveals no shattered
miniature bulbs or faulty
fuses. My string lights blew out
like nude flames.
Friendships are bright flares,
fiery-lights.

Did I forget to kindle them?

Unravelling

loneliness
is a spectre of fate who always looms.
she unknots the red strings of my woven youth,
every hug a stitch,
every lent hair-tie a stitch,
unpicked. unpicked. my thumb traces the slim
indent that circles
my left
wrist, familiarising itself with this familiar
indent of absence.

At the other end
of the playground your ponytail
swings.

The Sun (Reversed) in Tarot

we were all playthings once
trinkets among trinkets, tokens. Childhood
is a grownup's ghetto/haven – nostalgia. Tokens,
we were tokens.

"A child's pine for love is hinged on (insert
name here's) ability to love"
is a sentence.
The only frank one
I know. Hope is a grim dawn-yellow reaper
and disenchantment is her cloak. Yes

– even daylight can be dimmed like a cancerous
daffodil.
No cure. A wish
is always a blow, a burst dandelion,
a naked bulb without
its spindly seeds,
a dry well.

All Animals Have The Same Parts

Like a cherry you're careful to spit the pit
out of - this one pops
between your teeth. You sear her neck
as your work your way down, saving it for your
soup pot.
You fillet one breast, milk the other, flour her
arms
like protracted wings. On a low heat, you spit
roast her ribs
until tender. Grill her heart. Braise her cheeks,
turn her placenta
into a pill and eat her pussy
raw. Nothing is wasted,
you stuffed her jaw with an apple. It un-
latched.

Raise Daughters

whose gazes droop like petals
whose patience grows like shoots
with hearts like pollen
and tempers like roots.

We want beautiful bouquets.

Raise daughters with tongues like nectar
whose spines sway like reeds
with hair curled like florets
and palms open like leaves.

They want beautiful bouquets.

Amnion

*Neoprene is the insulating material used to
make spacesuits. It is inflated with oxygen
before astronauts leave their shuttles.

Embedded in space – viscous
like amniotic fluid,
potent gases bubble
into beginnings of things we name.
Multiply into cratered moons
and cratered planets, burning
stars and burning
suns – pools, puddles of light immersed
in a darkness that births
things brighter than artificial rays.

Entire worlds suspended
in matter that anchors
non-things lighter than hydrogen
and makes elements heavier
than uranium float.
Whole galaxies implanted
in - darkness: a uterine lining that fixes
celestial bodies
without breaking their fetal skin.

Darkness: closed eyes
that dissolve
the face behind the lips
I press my own against.
Darkness: fog hanging
in a room made strange
where we feel for the banister
of each other's bodies.
Darkness: we are groping, blind, naked
charting parts of ourselves
invisible to us.
Darkness: you jettison from
wet, wrinkled, blue – shrieking
out of lungs that inflate
like Neoprene.

Nakedness is Not Enough
with You

I arrived, bringing only my body
and her wide protruding hands. Please - unclasp
my fleshy costume, I ache
to sigh her off
like a sequined gown or second skin.
Undress me

Eight-Second Hugs

We respire, interlinking our ribcages.
Our chests hum. Hold me
longer – my collar bone will soften.
I'll be less brittle, less flesh, more marrow. I'll
remember
my contour, the swells
and
dips that map my body – are nooks for your
wrists
to settle into.
Feel for the marrow of me. Hold me
longer. None of us are all skin and bone.

Listening to Mariah Carey

Crescendos of thunder
drapes of rain – it is raging
outside. I am drifting…
wafting into a sunflower field carried –
moved by the chanteuse and her dulcet aria.
You are the monarchs of all flowers,
with your ruffs
of luminous mane
throned up there in the vast blue.
Faithfully you turn to face the yellow dwarf
ever attentive to our only star.
Ogling him from east to west – you have your
green backs to me
but I know your seeds,
like my skin,
are deepening their brown.
At dusk your petals will droop
and I will lumber
out of my daydream, just in time
to catch
her last refrain evaporating
into the electric electric mist.

After Letitia Chan (winner of 'Foyle Young Poets of the Year Award' 2016)

Hearing you at an open-mic night
somewhere
I'd recognise the lithe girlishness of your work,
its elasticity.
I'd trace the arc of your words as they bent
like umbrella tops.

Do you still write poems
about kneading dead skin into dough with the
balls of your palms.
Gingery, steaming poems.

Letitia –
If you never publish again
I hope you're still writing
poems. Become a posthumous poet.
Leave pages behind like ashes
I might use to craft a papier-mâché bust,
a body of your work.
An effigy to a lost poet might be remembered

the way I recite

'Making Glutenous Dumplings with My
Mother'.
Its sesame paste, its sleepless androgyny,
and then its dumplings that bubble like jilted
bodies
culminate in the potency of your last line

and the silence that followed.

www.ingramcontent.com/pod-product-compliance
Lightning Source LLC
Chambersburg PA
CBHW070730160726
48003CB00006BA/2434